SARAH STONE'S
UNSEEN WORLDS

SARAH STONE'S
UNSEEN WORLDS

A Rare Collection of 18th Century
Ornithological Watercolours

Errol Fuller & Craig Finch

IMPRESS–PUBLISHING, OXFORD

IMPRESS–PUBLISHING
32 East Street
Osney Island
Oxford
Oxfordshire
OX2 0AU

ISBN 978-1-912930-67-8

A CIP catalogue record for
this book is available from the
British Library

Designed by
Errol Fuller, Frankie Fuller, and
et al design consultants:
Prof. Phil Cleaver & Jenny Penny
Photography by Phil Connor
Printed and bound in Great Britain
by Pureprint

Half title: *Sarah's painting of a
Parakeet.*
Frontispiece: *An Amazon Parrot
with a Cockatoo. Signed 'Sarah Smith'
(Sarah's married name) and dated 1801.*
This page: *A view of the interior of the
Leverian Museum.*

for

E, M & M

AN INTRODUCTION TO THIS COLLECTION OF TWENTY-THREE WATERCOLOURS

The importance of Sarah Stone as an artistic recorder of significant and newly discovered items towards the end of the eighteenth century and the first part of the nineteenth has long been recognised, and her pictures are valued treasures in many museums around the world. Several hundred of her watercolours are recorded as existing in museum collections from which they will never emerge. But in private hands there remain very few. This is because, due to the great desire museums have shown for their acquisition, the vast majority of her work has been scooped up by institutions. This makes the discovery of a cache of 23 paintings still in private hands quite remarkable. Their existence as a collection is due to the fact that for almost 200 years they have been in the hands of Sarah's family and until recently they belonged to a descendant of hers, Patrick Dockar-Drysdale.

Almost certainly there is no chance of another collection of this kind or magnitude ever becoming available. All the pictures featured here are watercolours, which, of course, is the medium that Sarah used. All are in fine, unfaded condition and have been lovingly and carefully looked after during the many years that have elapsed since they were produced.

They span a considerable period of Sarah's working life. Although only some are actually dated, some are demonstrably early works, some come from a middle period and at least one is a very late painting. Of those that are not dated a rough idea of when the pictures were produced can be gleaned from their signatures; some are signed 'Sarah Stone' and some 'Sarah Smith' – which is how she styled herself after her marriage in 1789. The early pictures were certainly produced at the Leverian Museum when it was under the control of Ashton Lever and some of those signed under her married name were also painted using Leverian specimens.

A wide variety of species are featured, the majority being birds that inhabited recently visited places that were far from Europe, and had been brought back by the important exploratory expeditions that were occurring at the

Detail from Sarah Stone's painting of a Guinea Touraco

A portrait of Sarah by
Samuel Shelley (circa 1790).
Engraved for the
Universal Review *(1890)*
approximately 100 years
after it was drawn.

Opposite:
Yellow-throated Warbler

time. However, some, like the Goldfinch or the Dotterel, were depictions of more familiar European species.

Sarah's naming of her subjects (often handwritten at the top of the painting) can be problematic as the books that were in vogue at the time – and that she usually used for identification purposes – are now largely out of date and the names given are no longer used in modern ornithology. There are some that cannot be readily correlated with present-day identifications. Whether this is because they are hybrids, or whether they are birds that no longer exist, cannot always be said. There is no doubt, however, that each picture is an accurate rendition of what Sarah saw before her, so some must remain something of a mystery. Perhaps these were aberrant forms, which is why she chose to paint them, perhaps some were unusual sub-species or in some cases they show unusual immature plumages not typical of the adult bird.

It is clear that Sarah went on painting long after the dissolution of the Leverian collection so some of her paintings may have been produced at a surprisingly late date. Sometimes attempts have been made to date paintings in museum collections according to perceived stylistic changes or the use of greater or less detail in backgrounds etc., but such attributions are largely bogus. Sarah painted what she saw before her and painted it in a way that she thought best suited to her subject, rather than becoming a slave to whatever changes in style or taste advancing years might have encouraged. As a general rule the pictures remain remarkably consistent over the period of her active life. As far as this recently discovered set of 23 images is concerned, we know that they range in date from her earliest efforts, right up until 1837 near to the end of her life.

One interesting fact is revealed by the collection. This concerns the various kinds of paper that Sarah used. Although all the paper is of suitable quality, there is no consistency or continuity over the paper on which the images are painted. Presumably, this is due to the scarcity of good quality paper and the difficulty in finding paper exactly like that which she had used before. It is only by handling the collection as a whole that this becomes apparent.

The perfect state of preservation of these paintings clearly demonstrates the expertise and care she used in finding materials that would stand the test of time, and the care and treatment that they have received over the years.

SARAH STONE:
HER LIFE AND WORK

Sarah Stone lived in an age when the achievements of women – excepting those of the domestic variety – went largely disregarded, even entirely dismissed. Although many women of the era were talented watercolour painters, their efforts were usually confined to albums or at best allowed to decorate the walls of friends or family. Few enjoyed any degree of commercial success or widespread admiration. Discouraged, ignored or firmly instructed on their place in society, the odds were stacked against women no matter how considerable were their talents.

Sarah Stone proved to be one of the exceptions to such customs and ways of behaviour. In this she might be compared with the celebrated Mary Anning (1799–1847) who, at Lyme Regis in Dorset, kick-started the fashion for collecting fossils and gave it a certain scientific rigour, despite being a woman who came from the 'wrong side of the tracks'.

Sarah too enjoyed a success that went way beyond the expectations or hopes of most women of the day. Beautiful, determined, highly skilled and with a clear vision of what she hoped to achieve, she enjoyed commercial triumph at a comparatively early age, and this success continued for her whole life. Apart from her own personality traits, there were clearly a number of factors that combined to assist her in this.

Her natural talent was obviously essential to recognition of her ability. Then there was the fact that she married a successful man (and became known as Mrs Smith) who so admired her ability and so sympathised with her predicament that he actively encouraged the flair she showed and helped to promote her endeavours – rather than stand in her way, as many men of the time would have done. In fact, he was also a painter of some ability and in 1791, two years after their wedding, they were exhibiting together at exhibitions in London.

There was also the matter of the subjects she chose. These were mostly individual and highly detailed portraits of articles newly discovered and being brought back for the first time from far-flung corners of the globe – and in the process arousing intense curiosity and interest in certain sections of society. In addition to her suitability for rendering accurate and exquisite representations of these fascinating items, this selection of subject matter was probably crucial to her early success and she quickly became a specialist in making accurate

This painting of an Emu was made for John White's Journal of a Voyage to New South Wales *(1790), but Sarah was obliged to produce it by copying an anonymous work that had been drawn near Sydney in Australia. In the book it is erroneously labelled as a Cassowary but it is clearly an Emu.*

Opposite: *One of four images typical of the variety of work that Sarah produced – a bird, a shell, a mammal and two ethnographical items.*
A Silky Anteater.

A seashell (Bear's Paw Clam).

A Twelve-wired
Bird of Paradise.

images of preserved birds, mammals, fish, insects, seashells, fossils, minerals and ethnographical material.

Although she may not have realised it at the time, these images were to assume an importance to later generations far beyond just their actual beauty. When she was sitting in her chair studiously and conscientiously making two-dimensional images of the three-dimensional objects before her, she could never have had any real awareness that her pictures were to acquire a historical and scientific importance out of all proportion to their loveliness. For these paintings were to become visual records of significant historical specimens, many of which no longer exist, and some of which even vanished during her lifetime. A number were of specimens brought back by Captain Cook and some of these were recorded visually only by Sarah – and the items themselves are now lost or their whereabouts unknown.

So, Sarah Stone's works have become icons of a period when the horizons of what might be termed the 'enlightened world' were literally being rapidly expanded. The beauty of the images obviously facilitates this, as does their no-frills accuracy. But a vital ingredient to their immortality is the association that she formed with Sir Ashton Lever and his famous Leverian Museum. This permitted her seemingly unrestricted access to objects that had never been seen before, and in many cases items that would only exist for a comparatively short space of time.

How then did it all start? Sarah was the daughter of a man who painted and decorated fans. Due to the fashionable requirement at the time for such items, it is likely that his services were in some demand and that his family enjoyed a reasonable standard of living. It is also likely that the young Sarah learned from her father much about the nature of painting. Indeed, there is no record that she received any kind of formal artistic training other than the guidance she got from him. In order to satisfy his customers, the decorating of fans would have required precision and delicate skills and it seems likely that from an early age Sarah was assisting in the work – or at least observing how he went about things. Any tuition he gave would not have been restricted merely to the act of painting, but would also have included advice on the preparation of materials – the production of colours, the making of brushes, the importance of 'sizing' surfaces that were to receive paint etc.

Before she was 20 (in fact by the age of 17) Sarah was confident enough in her ability to believe that she could produce finished paintings of some worth. There seems to be no record of exactly how it came about, but at some point

Sarah Stone

Two Hawaiian feather heads probably brought to England on Cook's Third Voyage and once in the Leverian Museum. Painted circa 1783.

Opposite: *A Hawaiian chief's feather cape almost certainly brought to Britain on one of Cook's voyages.*

This page: *A view of the interior of the Leverian Museum with some of its visitors admiring exhibits.*

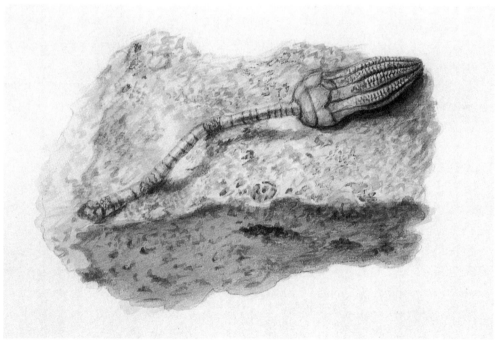

A fossil Crinoid (sea lily). An inscription on the reverse of this watercolour suggests that it is the very first painting Sarah ever produced for Ashton Lever.

she aroused the attention of Ashton Lever, then busily acquiring objects for his celebrated collection that was becoming known as the Leverian Museum. It is likely that, fascinated by the objects he owned (and having previously visited the museum), she approached him to ask if she might paint some of them. One can imagine her showing him some of her previous work and Sir Ashton, sufficiently impressed, agreeing to her proposal. At some point he would have properly appreciated her talent and actively commissioned her to produce images of his possessions. Whether he selected the items she was to paint or whether she did the choosing is not known but their artistic collaboration must have been a fairly easy-going and mutually friendly one, as it continued for years and she attended the collection to paint almost every day for a long, long time, in fact long after Sir Ashton himself had left the scene.

During this time, it is true to say that the majority of her subjects were birds, painted using as reference specimens preserved by the taxidermists of the day. Their standards were not always of the highest order, and often their products were riddled with anatomical inaccuracy, but Sarah painted whatever was in front of her, including any taxidermical flaws presented on the specimen itself.

A criticism of her painting that is sometimes made rests on the fact that the pictures depict any such faults with a great degree of accuracy and that she should have aspired to reproduce anatomical reality. But such criticism misses the point. Sarah's talent was that she copied whatever was in front of her, accurately and truthfully, and therein lies not only her paintings' charm but also their value. It is also true that she had no chance to assess anatomical reality as there was not necessarily an opportunity for her to see her subjects in living form – they often came from far, far away. These paintings might be regarded more accurately as 'still lives' rather than as attempts at what would be regarded today as lifelike 'bird paintings'.

In this respect her paintings might be compared with those of her French contemporary Jacques Barraband (1767–1809) who, like Sarah, was painting beautiful images of (usually exotic) birds from models supplied to him directly from specimens that were the handiwork of taxidermists. It should be remembered that the specimens both artists were working from were often of strange and exotic species that they had little hope of ever seeing in life. Birds of Paradise form a very good example of the problem that early taxidermists faced, along with those who used their products as reference. The arrangement of plumage in these creatures is often so extraordinary (and unlike anything to be found in European birds) that those who could never see the birds in life

Sarah's husband,
John Langdale Smith.

could not be expected to render them correctly. In terms of her private life it is apparent from contemporary accounts (and this is confirmed by existing portraits) that she was very attractive in appearance. A certain Lewis Allen – an artist who married Sarah's niece – described her thus for a journal known as the *Universal Review* in 1890, almost 50 years after her death. The article was published to promote an exhibition of Sarah's paintings that was happening in London during that year. Allen's description was of Sarah when she was more than 60 years of age:

She had all the best parts of beauty, a fine countenance, a good figure, and a pleasing address.

The year 1789 was a very eventful one for Sarah. She was 29 and unmarried but in this year she married a seaman, John Langdale Smith. At this time he was a midshipman but later he became a captain and from this period forward she usually signed her paintings 'Mrs Smith'.

Earlier in the year she had been approached by John White who was preparing one of the most important books of the age, the historically significant *Journal of a Voyage to New South Wales*. In addition to the written account it contained, the book was also to feature numerous plates picturing the hitherto unknown fauna of Australia.

An indication of Sarah's already considerable reputation is indicated by White's use of her name in his promotional advertising material. He boasted that his book would include:

A great variety of plates… copied from nature by Miss Stone.

He hardly bothered to mention other artists who contributed to the work! In fact she drew 49 plates for the book and there are at least two copies in existence in which the black and white engravings were hand-coloured by Sarah herself.

During 1795, she gave birth to a son, Henry Stone Smith (1795–1881) who was to father a large number of children.

Sarah Stone's output is extraordinary. She seems to have painted on most days of her comparatively long life and owing to their nature and the high standard of the materials she used (which doubtless was due at least in part to the instruction she had received from her father) many of her pictures have survived. An important reason for their survival is certainly down to the fact that many were acquired by museums around the world where they have been carefully curated and valued, and rarely exposed to daylight. The keenness of museums to acquire Sarah's watercolours renders the existence of her paintings in private hands today very rare and this makes this extraordinary collection of 23 pictures remarkable. There is unlikely to be another discovery of a similar selection both in quality and quantity.

Sarah died in 1844 of pneumonia. Her age at the time of death is given variously as either 82 or 83.

A watercolour (circa 1800) by Sarah's French contemporary Jacques Barraband who painted, as she did, using taxidermy specimens as models. In this case the species is a Red Bird of Paradise.

The frontispiece of John White's historically important Journal of a Voyage to New South Wales *(1890) to which Sarah became a major contributor.*

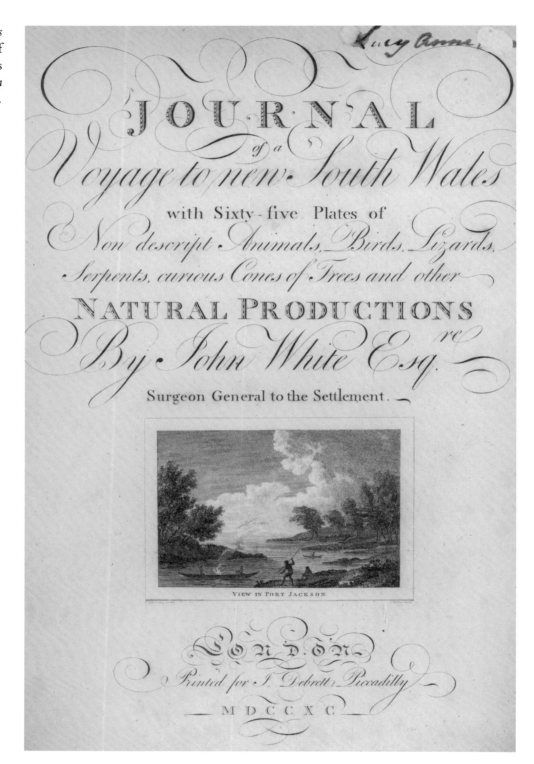

Lucy Anne

JOURNAL

of a

Voyage to new South Wales

with Sixty-five Plates of

Non descript Animals, Birds, Lizards,

Serpents, curious Cones of Trees and other

NATURAL PRODUCTIONS

By John White Esqre

Surgeon General to the Settlement.

VIEW IN PORT JACKSON.

LONDON

Printed for J. Debrett, Piccadilly

— M DCC XC —

One of the illustrations Sarah prepared for the book. This image was captioned: 'The Small Paraquet'.

SIR ASHTON LEVER
(1720–1788)
&
THE HISTORY OF THE
LEVERIAN MUSEUM

The importance of the Leverian Museum in Sarah Stone's life came in a variety of ways. First, it enabled her to achieve commercial success at an early age. Second, it provided her with, and exposed her to, rich and plentiful source material that was entirely suited to her artistic ability and nature. It was material that inspired her and material to which she was given free access. Third, due to its enormous celebrity as an institution it exposed her work to an appreciative public and set the tone and pattern for her whole life.

There is, therefore, no doubt that one of the factors making Sarah Stone so important and interesting is her early association with Ashton Lever and his Leverian Museum.

One may ask from today's perspective: why is this collection of material so celebrated by those who interest themselves in the formation and history of museums? The reasons are comparatively simple. The institution must be judged by the standards of its time, and at the end of the eighteenth century, museums were essentially things of the future, and what we might call 'actual' museums were rarities. The more typical collections were, and for centuries had been, private collections – assemblages of material put together by wealthy men to satisfy their own interests. These became known as 'cabinets of curiosities'. There are any number of famous examples – the collection of Olaus Wormius (1588–1654) in Denmark, for instance, or Rudolph II (1552–1612), Holy Roman Emperor and ruler of the Austro-Hungarian Empire. And in a sense Lever's collection began as one of these.

He seems to have been a man who was increasingly fascinated by the treasures that were arriving regularly in Europe from remote parts of the world. In this he had an advantage over his predecessors who were usually restricted to curiosities that had been found in the Northern Hemisphere; narwhal horns or mammoth bones etc. were typical deposits in their collections. Sometimes these men were lucky enough or rich and powerful enough to acquire objects

The stuffed dodo owned by Rudolph II painted by Georg Hoefnagel (circa 1603). This specimen may have been smoke damaged during a fire, accounting for its brownish colour.

Rudolph II painted by
Hans von Aachen
(circa 1600).

Opposite: *The interior of the*
Leverian Museum. This picture is
thought to be a copy of a painting
produced by Sarah Stone at the
time when Sir Ashton Lever was
thinking of disposing of his museum.
Her original painting, exhibited at
the Royal Academy under the title
Perspective View of Sir Ashton
Lever's Museum, *has been lost but*
this alleged copy remains.

from further afield. Rudolph II had, for instance, the remains of a dodo from Mauritius along with many other specimens from distant lands. However as a general rule such curiosities were comparatively few and far between.

Perhaps realising just what an advantageous position he was in, Lever became more and more entranced by the wealth of material that was becoming available. This was, of course, due to the technological advantages that were making it possible for explorers from Europe and North America to venture to places that were previously inaccessible. Such exploratory voyages were becoming increasingly frequent, often backed by governments and the interests of developed nations.

At some point an idea must have occurred to Lever that had only occurred to a comparative few of his predecessors. This was to create a facility that was not just for his private amusement, but could be opened up to the public at large – in other words, a museum! Not only did this have the advantage of increasing his personal status and celebrity, it also raised the possibility of providing something of an income, as visitors would be expected to pay for admission. At the opening to the public of his museum, the admission charge was pitched at 10 shillings and sixpence, a considerable sum by the standards of the day.

So, the Leverian Museum was founded and it grew to become larger and larger. Some degree of its eventual size can be formed not only by existing pictures of its interior but also by the fact that when it was finally disbanded in 1806 the auction sale at which the items were dispersed took place over almost 60 days!

Ashton Lever was clearly a man who was fascinated by natural history from an early age. He formed an enormous aviary that apparently housed some 4,000 living birds at his home near Manchester, but at the age of 30 his attention appears to have been directed to the acquisition of items that didn't move! On a visit to Dunkirk he bought a collection of shells. Whether or not this was his first purchase of what we might term 'curiosities' is not known, but it certainly seems to have encouraged him in this direction.

Before long he had acquired thousands of items and he made the decision to open a museum to the public. The place for such an enterprise was obviously London, and as a venue he selected Leicester House, a large property situated in what is now Leicester Square. The rent for this property was £600 per year, which gives some idea of the scale of the enterprise.

During 1778, just a year or so after the grand opening, Sarah began working at the museum (which she seems to have done on an almost daily basis). In the

same year Ashton Lever was granted a knighthood by George III and from then on became Sir Ashton Lever.

Three years later he acquired thousands of specimens from Cook's Third Voyage and Sarah painted many of them. It is likely that these acquisitions added greatly to the celebrity of the museum, not least because of morbid curiosity surrounding the circumstances of Cook's death in Hawaii.

During the following year (1784) Sir Ashton placed advertisements that advised interested parties that in addition to its regular exhibitions there would be a display of more than a thousand of Sarah Stone's paintings. Not only does this indicate the sheer volume of work she had been doing at the museum, but it also confirms her renown as an artist. The advertisement states:

Above one thousand different articles, executed by Miss Stone, a young lady who is allowed by all artists to have succeeded in the effort beyond all imagination.

So fond of her paintings had Sir Ashton become that after the exhibition he removed them to his home near Manchester.

But times were becoming increasingly difficult for Sir Ashton. Almost 250 years after the events it is easy to speculate on the nature of his problems. Presumably, his spending habits had grown out of hand and he was facing financial turmoil. Attendances were down, forcing him to halve the admission fee; the rent on the property was becoming an exorbitant burden and Lever came to the painful decision to part with ownership of his museum. To decide on the best way to proceed presented a problem and presumably feeling that no single person would have the inclination plus the wherewithal to buy it, he made a strange plan. Having been turned down by the British Museum to which he had offered his collection at what he considered a reasonable price, he took the decision to sell it by lottery. During 1784 he obtained permission to do this, but this procedure required an Act of Parliament before it could go ahead. It wasn't until March 1786 that the lottery took place.

Perhaps feeling that the entire museum would be broken up, Sarah painted a detailed picture of the interior, a painting that was exhibited at the Royal Academy titled *Perspective View of Sir Ashton Lever's Museum*. This painting seems now to be lost and all trace of it is gone, but what is believed to be a copy by an unknown hand exists at the British Museum (*see* p.27). This painting with its view that extends through one room to several others gives some idea of the scale of Lever's collection.

A famous painting of Captain James Cook by Nathaniel Dance-Holland painted circa 1775 just before Cook left on his fatal Third Voyage.

[29]

Thirty-six thousand tickets were offered for sale at the price of £1 each, but by the day of the lottery draw only 8,000 had actually been sold. With 28,000 tickets still in his rightful possession, Sir Ashton – believing he had a good chance of winning – took the gambler's bet and allowed the draw to go ahead. It took place at the Guildhall on 24th March and unfortunately Sir Ashton's hopes didn't come off; despite the odds in his favour his rash move didn't work. The winning ticket belonged to a Mr James Parkinson, apparently a law stationer although some records state that he was a barrister.

For some weeks, no one came forward to claim the prize. Apparently the winning ticket had been purchased by Mr Parkinson's wife, who had died before the lottery draw took place. Parkinson only discovered the ticket while going through his late wife's effects. There was considerable public sympathy for Lever and many felt that under the circumstances Parkinson should have let Sir Ashton continue in possession of his museum, and it seems that the new owner was generally disliked.

On the subject of his disappointment Lever told a German friend, Sophie von La Roche:

I come here daily to view these objects which I view as old friends… For they will be in strange hands… It was a passion of mine to possess all nature's wonders, no expense was spared. I have spent over a million on it and now that I am old I find that I have hardly enough to be able to live in comfort.

He retired to his property near Manchester and died suddenly in early 1788, perhaps of a broken heart or, as was whispered, from a dose of poison that had been self-administered.

Parkinson, meanwhile, had taken full possession of the museum, as was his right, and at first tried to sell it. In this he failed, but he then quickly adapted to his new role in life.

Realising that the rent for Leicester House was unsustainable he moved the museum to a cheaper part of town. The spot he chose was known as the Rotunda and it was situated just to the south of Blackfriars Bridge. The entrance fee was once again halved, this time to 2 shillings and sixpence.

Parkinson remained the sole owner for 20 years during which time he promoted his possession widely. However, the attraction of the museum waned, something not helped by its situation in an unfashionable area. By 1806 Parkinson felt the need to sell and offered the whole to the government,

One of several magnificent trompe l'oeil paintings made by French painter Alexandre-Isidore Leroy de Barde (1777–1828) at the Leverian Museum. The paintings were undertaken when the museum was under the ownership of James Parkinson probably around 1800. They are now in the Louvre.

[31]

Frontispiece of the catalogue of the first part of the Leverian Museum sale.

Catalogue

OF THE

LEVERIAN MUSEUM,

PART I.

INCLUDING THE FIRST EIGHT DAYS' SALE.

———

*** THE REMAINING PARTS WILL BE PUBLISHED WITH ALL POSSIBLE SPEED.

———

THE SALE

OF

THE ENTIRE COLLECTION

(By Messrs. KING and LOCHEE,)

WILL COMMENCE

On MONDAY, the 5th of MAY, 1806, at Twelve o'Clock,

In the Building now occupied by

THE MUSEUM.

———

CATALOGUES to be had (price 1s.) at the Place of Sale; at Messrs. *King* and *Lochée*'s, (the Auctioneers) and at *Hayden's* Printing-Office, Brydges-Street, Covent-Garden.

Hayden, Printer, 4, Brydges Street, Covent Garden.

A painting by Ramsay Richard Reinagle now in the Yale Center for British Art, Paul Mellon Collection, New Haven, Connecticut. The picture was produced circa 1800 and is titled Mr. Thomson, Animal and Bird Preserver to the Leverian and British Museums. *It is likely, therefore, that this is a portrait of Thomas Thomson, the man commissioned to bid by Lord Stanley on his behalf at the Leverian Auction. Thomson is shown examining a Bird of Paradise, presumably to determine whether or not it was suitable for the purposes of taxidermy.*

however he was turned down. So he adopted the idea of selling by auction and the still famous Leverian Auction took place. It is interesting to note that even to this day it is always known as the Leverian Auction, never the Parkinson Sale despite the fact that Parkinson owned the collection for far longer than Lever ever did!

The sale took place on the premises of the museum itself and began on Monday 5th March 1806. Fortunately, annotated copies of the sale exist and these list many of the buyers, but the present-day resting places of many of the objects have been lost and many have simply vanished.

Although so many objects are now in the lost or 'whereabouts unknown' categories, the buyers of a considerable number are known. Edward Donavan (1768–1837), a well-known naturalist of the time and producer of books, purchased multiple lots as did representatives of the Vienna Museum; these Viennese lots remain safely in Vienna to this day. Another buyer was Lord Stanley, Earl of Derby (1752–1834) from Knowsley near Liverpool. Stanley commissioned a taxidermist and dealer named Thomas Thomson to bid for him and this man may be the subject of a portrait in oils by Ramsay Richard Reinagle (1775–1862) that is now in the collection at Yale. Although Yale once believed this to be the portrait of another man, this attribution has been shown to be bogus (*see* Attenborough and Fuller, *Drawn From Paradise*, 2012, p.54).

The significance of the Leverian sale in terms of the work of Sarah Stone lies in the importance and value it has given it, for so many of the items have vanished over time and only her paintings remain to immortalise them. Indeed, during the 20th century scientists, historians and researchers have increasingly leaned upon her watercolours to match them up and give insight into many of the items that remain and, of course, many of those that have vanished between 1806 and today.

TWENTY-THREE
WATERCOLOURS

BORNEAN PEACOCK PHEASANT
Polyplecton schleiermacheri

Signed *Sarah Smith* at the bottom of the image,
with a thin black border.
SIZE : 49.5 × 40 cm — 19½ × 15¾ inches

The origin of this spectacular watercolour presents something of a mystery. The signature (Sarah Smith) makes it clear that the picture was painted at some period after Sarah's marriage in 1789, but curiously the species was not scientifically described until 1877 – long after her death.

Even today it rarely occurs in captivity and how she came by the specimen she painted is unknown. It may have been in the Leverian collection or she may have come by it after the museum was dispersed.

However, despite the pheasant's spectacular and decorative appearance, the specimen she worked from does not seem to have been fully mature as it lacks some of the features of the mature male plumage. Interestingly, the picture features a fully rendered background, which is not always the case with her paintings.

Even today this is a very little-known species, restricted to Borneo, and it is regarded as threatened. There are a number of related species with similar 'eye' spots but most of these show a plumage that is grey in colour rather than brown.

YELLOW-THROATED
WARBLER
Setophaga dominica

Signed *Sarah Stone 1784* at the bottom of the image with an
inscription at the top that reads: *yellow throated Warbler
Gen. Syn 4, page 497* [or perhaps *437*].
SIZE: 35 × 25 cm − 13 ¾ × 9 ¾ inches

Although this is listed as a Yellow-throated Warbler, it is
certainly not a typical example of the species. However,
the careful way in which it is painted indicates that Sarah
was observing the preserved bird in front of her with great
accuracy.

The reference in the inscription to 'Gen. Syn' indicates that
she had seen the species listed in John Latham's standard
work of the time *A General Synopsis of Birds* which was
published in several volumes between 1781 and 1785. Her
reference to (volume) 4 can be misleading as the work is
sometimes bound in three volumes, sometimes six.

The date of the painting (1784) indicates that the specimen
was almost certainly in the Leverian Museum.

Yellow-throated Warbler. Gen. Syn. 4. p. 487?

Sarah Stone 1784

YELLOW-HEADED
AMAZON PARROT
Amazona ochrocephala oratrix

Signed *Sarah Smith* at the bottom of the image,
with a thin black border.
SIZE : 36 × 30.5 cm – 14 ¼ × 12 inches

This parrot (usually called the Yellow-headed Amazon)
is now regarded as a sub-species of the Yellow-crowned
Amazon, a sub-species that often seems to hybridise with
closely related birds.

Even in Sarah's time the species, which has long been very
popular as a pet, would have been readily available and she
may have produced this picture using a living bird as a model
– a factor that for her is quite unusual. That she depicted the
bird looking curiously, or greedily, at a fly indicates that this
might have been the case. Certainly, she would have seen
living examples of the species.

Sarah Smith

BLACK-FACED GRASSQUIT
Melanospiza bicolor

Signed *Sarah Stone 1780* at the bottom of the image with a
faint inscription at the top: *Bahamas Finch, Catesby pl.37;
Gen Syn, 3, p.300.*
SIZE: 35 × 25 cm — 13¾ × 9¾ inches

The identification of the bird featured in this watercolour is
problematic.

Sarah's identification in her written inscription is based on
a reference in Mark Catesby's *Natural History of Carolina,
Florida and the Bahamas Islands (1729–1732)* and another in
John Latham's *General Synopsis of Birds* (1781–1785). However, since the time of Catesby's writing the placing of the
species in modern-day systematics has changed enormously.
It is no longer regarded as a Finch (which is how Sarah had
classified it) but is now seen as a rather aberrant, and very
variable, member of the Tanager family. She also believed
it to be confined to the Bahamas, but the species occurs in
various parts of the Caribbean and northern South America.

The date of the painting indicates that the subject was in
the Leverian Museum.

Sarah Stone - 1780

YELLOW-HEADED
AMAZON PARROT
Amazona ochrocephala oratrix
WITH
HYBRID COCKATOO

Signed *Sarah Smith 1801* at the bottom of the image.
SIZE: 44.5 × 37 cm — 17½ × 14½ inches

The upper bird in this painting of an Amazon Parrot is a virtual copy of the Parrot in the watercolour previously featured where it is looking at a fly. There are only one or two very minor changes.

Both are signed 'Sarah Smith' so both were produced after her marriage; although only one is dated, it seems likely that both pictures were painted around the same time.

The plumage of the Cockatoo which the Amazon is interacting with in this image does not conform to any known species. It appears to be a hybrid between a Sulphur-crested Cockatoo (*Cacactua galerita*) and one of its close relatives of which there are several.

DOTTEREL
Eudromias morinellus

Signed *Sarah Stone* on the bottom border
and inscribed *Dotterel* on the upper border
with *Gen. Syn.* reference.
SIZE: 23 × 26 cm —9 × 10¼ inches

This species is a common European bird and, unlike most of
her subjects, Sarah would have had the opportunity to see
individuals in life.

The watercolour depicts a bird changing from its winter
plumage into the plumage it shows in the summer; in fact
the change has almost completely taken place.

The watercolour is slightly unusual in that it has a border
which Sarah has used for her signature and inscription.

GUINEA TOURACO

Tauraco persa

Signed *Sarah Smith* on the branch at the
bottom of the image.
SIZE: 31.5 × 24.5 cm — 12¼ × 9¾ inches

This watercolour of a Touraco from West Africa is almost
identical to the watercolour following. Neither are dated
and it is likely that both were produced at around the same
time using the same mounted bird as a model.

GUINEA TOURACO
Tauraco persa

Signed *S. Smith* on the branch at the bottom of the image,
with a black border.
SIZE: 34 × 30 cm — 13 ¼ × 11 ¾ inches

Although depicted facing in the opposite direction and
looking straight ahead, this image is very similar to the
previous watercolour and it is likely that both paintings
were produced using the same model even though the pose
of the head is different.

Signed *S. Smith* on the branch at the bottom of the image.
On the reverse of the painting these words are written:
Uncle Smith's Mother. Sarah Smith about 1837
SIZE: 18 × 10.5 cm — 7 × 4¼ inches

It has proved impossible to identify either of these Parakeets which are far from identical. Perhaps both are hybrids. Although such a late image in terms of Sarah's work, this painting seems to have had an early provenance that is different from the rest of the pictures shown here and at some stage it passed through the hands of a dealer, whose label is pictured below.

SLATY EGRET
Egretta vinaceigula

Signed *Sarah Stone 1792* at the bottom of the image.
SIZE: 40 × 29 cm — 15¾ × 11½ inches

The identification of this bird is somewhat tentative as there are several kinds of related herons with sub-species that closely resemble this image.

One peculiarity concerning the picture relates to the signature. It is clearly marked 'Sarah Stone 1792' but after her marriage in 1789 Sarah signed herself 'Sarah Smith', seemingly as a matter of course. Presumably, she simply forgot her new name for an instant at the time of writing, or perhaps a customer wanted the painting signed in the name by which she was then better known.

The date of 1792 means that this picture was not produced for Ashton Lever (as he was dead by this time) although it may well have been a depiction of a specimen in the Leverian collection, which was then owned by James Parkinson. It may have been comissioned by Parkinson himself or maybe for a private client.

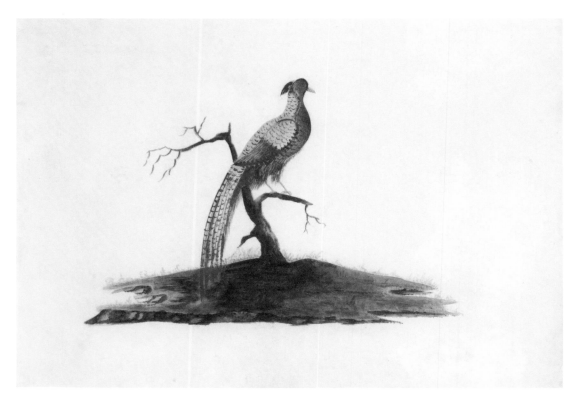

UNIDENTIFIED PHEASANTS

Unsigned.
SIZE: 19 × 27 cm — 7½ × 10½ inches

These two paintings present a variety of problems. They both appear to be images of some kind of exotic pheasant but they do not quite conform to any known species. This is not necessarily significant as pheasant species frequently hybridise.

The two paintings are very similar, however they are not quite identical, and there are several small, almost insignificant differences.

Perhaps the most extraordinary aspect of the pair is that one was stuck to the back of the other, and it is only by the skill of a conservator that they were separated. Whatever this means cannot now be said and the fact that they are unsigned and undated serves only to increase the enigma.

BARN OWL
Tyto alba

Signed *Sarah Smith* at the bottom of the image,
with a black border.
SIZE : 44.5 × 36 cm – 17½ × 14¼ inches

This remarkable picture shows a familiar British bird and
it is therefore unlikely to have had a connection with the
Leverian collection.

The image is unusual in the detailed manner in which the
Owl's perching place is depicted and the fully realised sky
behind the subect. Such detail is rarely shown in Sarah's
paintings. Why she went to so much additional trouble must
remain a mystery, but it makes this complex image a very
curious and desirable watercolour.

NUTHATCH sp.

Signed *Sarah Stone* at the bottom of the image
and inscribed *Nuthatch Gen Syn 2 p.654* at the top.
Also inscribed *Sitta surinamensis* [?].
SIZE : 35 × 25.5 cm — 13 ¾ × 10 inches

This watercolour certainly seems to show a species of
Nuthatch (of which there are a number living throughout
the world) but it does not quite correlate with any species
known today. Nor does the Latin name scribbled at the top
of the image match any name in modern use. So the image
remains something of a mystery.

DEMOISELLE CRANE
Anthropoides virgo

Signed *Sarah Smith* at the bottom of the image,
with a black border.
SIZE: 36 × 30.5 cm — 14¼ × 12 inches

This striking watercolour shows a Demoiselle Crane, which
was probably a fairly familiar species even in Sarah's lifetime
as it is highly migratory and sometimes occurs in England.

DARTFORD WARBLERS
Sylvia undata

Signed *Sarah Stone 1780* at the bottom of the image.
Inscribed at the top:
Dartford Warblers Motacilla dartfordensis Linn.
Gen Syn, 4 p.405.
SIZE: 35 × 25 cm — 13¾ × 9¾ inches

The watercolour shows a male bird (above) and a female (below). The species occurs in southern England but here it is at the northern extremity of its range. For this reason it has suffered from harsh winters to which it is ill-adapted, and at one point in time (1960s) there were only a handful of pairs in existence in the British Isles. It has made something of a recovery and, although still rare in Britain, fears for its future have decreased.

Whether Sarah chose to paint it because it was rare in her time is not easy to determine, however although it is not among her earliest paintings it was certainly produced at a relatively young age and at a time when she was working at the Leverian.

Dartford Warblers Gen: Syn: 4 p. 435   Motacilla Dartfordiensis Lin.

Sarah Stone 1788

GUIANAN COCK
OF THE ROCK
Rupicola rupicola

Unsigned.
SIZE: 26.5 × 26.5 cm — 10½ × 10½ inches

This image portrays a female of the species. Although the male has the same striking crest of feathers, it is a very bright orange in colour and so looks almost entirely different in appearance. Presumably Sarah didn't have a male specimen to hand; due to its spectacular colouring she would almost certainly have chosen to depict it. However, there are many images of the orange male but very few of the female bird — which makes this a painting of especial interest.

CARIB GRACKLE
Quiscalis lugubris

Signed *Sarah Stone 1785* on the branch at the bottom
of the image.
SIZE: 43 × 33 cm — 17 × 13 inches

The identification of this bird as a female Carib Grackle is
by no means certain as the plumage is so generalised. It is
simply the most likely candidate. There are no written clues
as sometimes occurs in pencil at the top of Sarah's images.
The species is common in parts of northern South America
and the Caribbean.

The date of the image indicates that it was probably one
of the last watercolours which Sarah painted at the Leverian
Museum while it was still under the control of Sir Ashton
Lever. It may, therefore, have been painted for his personal
collection. Unlike the other pictures in the collection, this
one is painted on rather thick card.

GOLDEN EAGLE
Aquila chrysaetos
WITH
COMMON BRONZEWING
Phaps chalcoptera

Signed *Sarah Smith 1806* at the bottom of the image.
SIZE : 46 × 55 cm — 18 × 21 ½ inches

This watercolour of one Golden Eagle being challenged by another presents something of an enigma – the prey item is a Bronze-winged Pigeon, an Australian species that Golden Eagles (being birds of the Northern Hemisphere) would never be exposed to! Perhaps Sarah found the opportunity to introduce an exotic bird into the painting too tempting to resist.

The date of 1806 may have significance for this is the year in which the Leverian collection was dispersed by auction. Possibly Sarah painted this at the museum just before it was broken up, or perhaps (after the dispersal) she was turning to painting dramatic specimens that – being native British species – were a little easier to come by.

WHITE-BROWED ROBIN-CHAT
Cossypha heuglini

Signed *Sarah Stone* at the bottom of the image.
Inscribed at the top: *Tanager*
Gen. Syn p.218
SIZE: 44 × 33 cm — 17¼ × 13 inches

Although Sarah was of the opinion that this bird was
a Tanager, it seems far more likely that it is what is
now called a White-browed Robin-chat, a common
species from East, Central and Southern Africa.

RUFOUS TREEPIE
Dendrocitta vagabunda

Unsigned.
SIZE: 21 × 16.5 cm — 8 ¼ × 6 ½ inches

The Rufous Treepie is a spectacular species from India and other parts of Southeast Asia. Unfortunately, without a date or any written details at the top edge of the image we have no idea why and under what circumstances Sarah painted this watercolour. Presumably it was a specimen at the Leverian Museum and it was one of the pictures Sarah painted for Sir Ashton Lever himself.

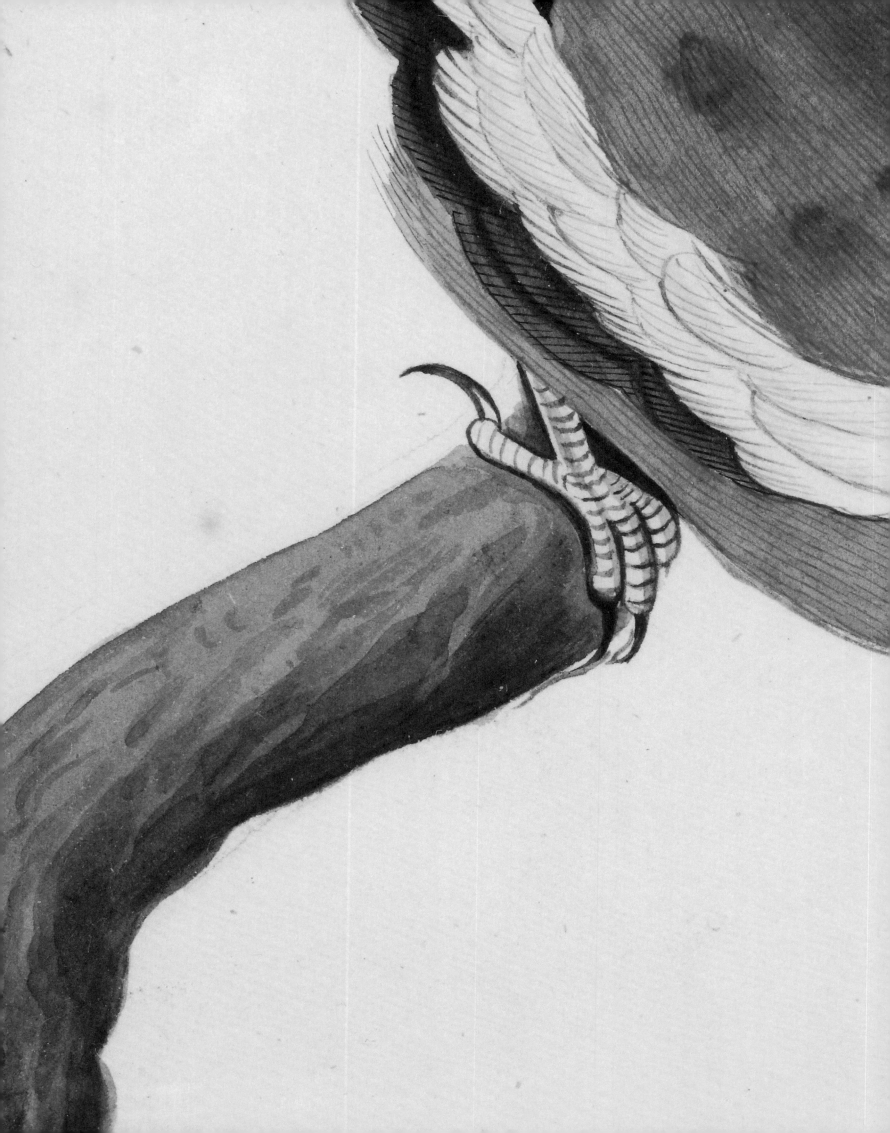

GOLDFINCH
Carduelis carduelis

Signed *Sarah Stone* on the orange border at the bottom
of the image.
Inscribed on the top border: *Common Goldfinch*
Gen Syn 5 p.281 Fringilla
carduelis Lin.
SIZE: 23.5 × 29.5 cm —9¼ × 11½ inches

The choice of subject for this painting, being a common
British bird, is slightly unusual for Sarah. Presumably she
was drawn to it by the species' bright, striking colours. The
use of an orange border is also a somewhat unusual feature.

Being signed 'Sarah Stone' rather than 'Sarah Smith' it
is clearly a fairly early work, although being undated it is
impossible to gauge just how early.

Sarah Stone

PARTRIDGE
Perdix perdix

Signed *Mrs Smith, Smith Square, West London*
and *J. , Mattias* on a painted trompe l'œil label.
Also signed *Sarah Smith* on the bottom border.
With a wood grain effect and a brown border
on one side and the bottom.
SIZE : 38 × 28 cm — 15 × 11 inches

This watercolour is most unusual in a number of ways that
may even be unique in Sarah's work; certainly these features
are highly uncommon. The painting shows a bird hanging
dead, pictured against a wood grain effect.

The painted and signed tied label at the top of the image
indicates that this is an attempt at trompe l'œil. The image
also seems to be a colloboration between Sarah Smith and
J. Mattias. Perhaps the unusual signature (*Mrs Smith*) was
designed to show that she was a respectable married woman
rather than having any obvious attachment to J. Mattias
other than in a professional artistic sense. The picture also
has an incomplete brown border on one side and another
to the bottom. Being incomplete and giving a shadow-like
look, perhaps they were intended to heighten the trompe
l'œil effect.

ACKNOWLEDGMENTS

The Sarah Stone book could not have been possible without the following important people in no particular order. To Errol Fuller, a friend, writer and artist, renowned collector, follower of snooker, boxing and other 'slightly' disreputable sports! This book would not have been made without his enthusiasm and scholarship. Edric Van Vredenburgh, for alerting me to the existence of the watercolours, and for his continued friendship and support over the past thirty years. To James Gascoigne of Pureprint Group. Louise Drover, conservator, for her patience and ability to meet my often extreme deadlines. Philip Connor, photographer, for twenty-two years of continued collaboration, discussions about lighting, shadows and angles, guitars and classic cars. Prof. Phil Cleaver and Jenny Penny at *et al design* studio, for their continued calming influence and belief that everything is possible and anything is achievable, it is just a matter of 'great design'! Richard Barnden for his ever professional framing. Adrian Finch, for co-ordinating the logistics, very often with tight schedules and always making them happen and run smoothly.

Finally to Elisabetta, Maddalena and Marta, thank you for your continued support, encouragement and enthusiasm since the outset of this exciting discovery in 2022 and developing those ideas and thoughts of a book, helping to make them become a reality. Your rightful reminders that this whole project is in support of those female artists who have struggled for centuries to break through, and how casting a light upon Miss Sarah Stone, and her extraordinary abilities in an age when it was so rare to find many contemporaries, underlines just how significant Sarah's body of work was at the time, scientifically, artistically, and as a permanent record of rare newly discovered species within the museum, prior to the dispersal auction of 1806. Seeing the world 'through your eyes', having a female perspective, observing, listening, is a true privilege, an insight into the daily struggles which are encountered in the 21st century. Although light years away from those experienced by Sarah Stone over 200 years ago, those comparisons are ever present. This book is dedicated to Sarah's memory, and all female artists, before and since, whose art is equal to any other art in whichever medium, size or genre. Art is without gender, without geographic or religious boundaries. Art is for anyone and everyone.   CF

'There are no rules. That is how art is born, how breakthroughs happen. Go against the rules or ignore the rules. That is what invention is about'. Helen Frankenthaler 1928–2011